GW01080025

The 7 Secrets to football success for junior and youth players. A guide to unlocking your footballing genius

- Learn exactly the same principles that have helped top professional players get to the top!

- This clear, simple and proven "Blueprint", if followed will ensure you become the best that you can be.

- Develop the "Power Habits" of "Genius and Success", that make your journey to success, faster, easier, and much more enjoyable.

- Learn how to harness the power of your greatest resource…YOU!

This book is "The Guide" to help junior and youth players unleash the massive potential of their mental, emotional and physical capabilities.

Praise for the 7 secrets book of football success for young players

"The 7 secrets of football success for young players is a must read for any young footballer wanting to improve their mind-set as well as their game. This enjoyable readable book, breaks down success in 7 easy to follow steps and encourages players to take responsibility for their own choices and development. This book can change the way young people think about themselves and make a difference in their game and in their life"

…Rob Josephs – Coordinator of student participation and leadership TLA Woodard Academy School

"I have always believed that the game of football can benefit children of all ages in both their personal and academic life. It teaches the life skills necessary to adopt a disciplined, respectful and fair approach to everyday situations. However the key for any coach is to find and adopt a strategy that helps to maintain their young players' motivation towards learning and development; to always strive for improve-ment. The 7 secrets to football success for young players is a valuable resource to help frame such a strategy which, I should imagine, any coach would find both insightful and useful."

…Peter Saywell – Managing Director – Saywell International

"If parents, coaches and teachers sit down and read this book with children there is the potential to transform attitudes and achievement in football. Much more than this, there is an opportunity for these core values to transfer into everyday life and change approaches, thinking and life chances. That is a very big impact for such a small book!"

…Janet Llewelyn, Headteacher, St. Mary's CofE School

"This book is excellent at providing the true understanding of a sports psychology philosophy with football which often gets missed with children. It is not only motivation-al, better still, it offers tips for kids to practice which means it provides the perfect formula for improvement: insight + action = positive change/ success. Mark has supported the teaching with strap line quotes to reinforce the message, which children can also apply to all aspects of their life. All in all a really valuable book for kids and parents to read in order to activate the 'successful inner footballer and team player."

…Andrea Chatten Lead Children's Behavioural Psychologist Consultant at Unravel and author of The Blinks

This short book is about a lot more than just the sport itself. It explores the core values that underpin great team work and promotes the development of the 'whole player' both on and off the pitch. An easy and accessible read for children, parents and teachers.

…Helen Morris, Headteacher, Summerlea CP School

The 'Seven Secrets To Football Success For Young Players' is an easy to read guide, giving succinct and memorable advice for players at all stages. It covers keys aspects of a players approach to football including their mentality, health and education, much of which is also universal advice for success in life. It is an excellent exemplar for players to make sure that they are fully prepared come match day when they step over the white line. A must read for all foot-ballers with ambition.

…Paul Deller, Head of Football, Christ's Hospital School

About the Author:

Mark Beauchamp is a professional speaker, UEFA "A" licence coach and director of the multiple award winning Pro Coaching Football Academy. In this book Mark captures the very essence of the disciplines and principles young players must follow in order to enjoy success not only as players but as people to. This book is a must read for junior and youth players along with their coaches, managers, parents, teachers and friends.

Printed by Baker Press Limited. www.bakerpress.com

Acknowledgements

Thank you for buying, but most importantly reading this book. The intention when writing this book was to share a collective knowledge base with people who could put the knowledge to best use, and enhance both the game, others and themselves.

The book is dedicated to my Hero...my Dad! The person who started it all. A special mention goes naturally to my family – Thank you. Amanda, Amelie, "our Mam", Min & Eddie, The Edwards's and Beauchamp North. Go team Beauchamp! I love you all xxx

This book is made possible by the incredible people with whom I am honoured to work alongside at Pro Coaching Football Academy. The coaches, players and parents are my biggest teachers without question.

The "Multiple Award Winning" Pro Coaching Football Academy Team are:
Tom Henton, Dan McIlwain, Ben Green, Mike Gillam, Tom Cosham, Liam Embleton, James Binfield, Alex Campbell, Ben Henton, Will Sparrow, Phil Gatland, James Butcher, Ben Pinar, Holly Marsh, Matt Ansell, Amanda Beauchamp and Jody Buckman.

I sincerely hope that you find value in this book and the subsequent "Players, Coaches and Parents Bookshelf series"

Mark Beauchamp
P.S. I draw your attention to the two charities below.

Care for the family

Care for the Family is a registered charity and has been working to strengthen family life since 1988. Their aim is to promote strong family relationships and to help those who face family difficulties. They provide parenting, relationship and bereavement support through events, resources, courses, training and volunteer networks across the UK.

www.careforthefamily.org.uk

Sports Family

Sports Family is a brand new charity set up to help support and enrich the lives of players, parents, guardians and the educators of young sports people. Their key aims are to provide education, promote knowledge, best practices and support to players and the key members of a young sports persons "team". This support will be provided through events, training and coaching sessions, school workshops, and resources available throughout the West Sussex area.

www.sportsfamily.org.uk

"*It's not just about football,
it's about life!* **"**

...Stan – Year 5

CONTENTS

The 7 secrets of football success

Well done for even taking the time to read this short but powerful book. Did you know that most people who buy a book never finish it! What is the point in that?

This book isn't the answer to everything but it does have some really great information to help you on your journey to become the best that you can be.

Take note of this important point; everything thing in this book is connected. Which is great news because part of the magic of studying this book, is that as you use all of the secrets together, they become much more powerful than if you just used one or two of the secrets on their own.

It is very much like a football team playing together. The team are much more powerful when the whole team work together.

The coaches at Pro Coaching Football Academy teach players that whenever something new is being learned (which is every day, we never stop learning!), we put whatever we learn through a little thinking machine called "THE MODEL T"*

Here is the Model T in action…

1. Try it
2. Test it
3. Tweak it
4. Trust it or Trash it
5. Teach it

While you are studying the 7 secrets to football success think about the Pro Coaching Football Academy thinking machine the Model T and see what happens.

It takes a little time to learn how to use the Model T but you will definitely find it very valuable.

The concepts in this book are simple but it would be valuable for parents, coaches, managers and teachers to talk about the chapters with players.

Contact us to attend a workshop or get learning materials and resources to make the process of learning the 7 secrets to football success a joy.

Ok, let's get straight into the action and kick off with success secret #1…

CHAPTER 1
ATTITUDE

Success secret #1
Attitude

There is a very old saying that says…

> ## " *Your attitude determines your altitude.* "

Which is just a fancy Dan way of saying if you have a good attitude you will be more successful.

Let's have a look at if there is any truth in that saying. Let's take a look at two players who play in the same team but have very different attitudes…

One player is always moaning and complaining about everyone and everything. The other player is generally happy and enjoys playing fairly with their friends.

The second player is the type of player who gets on with the things that will help them improve, even if those things are a bit tough.

Which player do you think will eventually become a really good all-round football player?

We all know the answer, don't we?

It seems to make sense that the player who moans about everyone and everything will probably get so fed-up that they will give up.

What other things do you think might happen to the player that moans about everyone and everything?

Let's ask ourselves some questions...

1. What type of people do you like to be around most of the time?

2. Which people would you want around if your team was losing; the moaners and complainers or the people who want to try and make things better?

We know which people we want around and to be around.

Are you a zapper or a sapper?

Energy **"Zappers"** tend to give those people around them good positive energy...a Buzz!

Energy **"Sappers"** tend to be those people who drain your energy and create negative energy...a Buzz Kill!

Which person do you think would be most likely to be most successful as a football player?
Ask your coach, "How's my attitude?"

Attitude check

Ok, let's have an attitude check and find out how you are doing with your attitude!

Imagine your coach (or your Mum/Dad/who ever looks after you), have asked you to doing something that may not be the most interesting thing in the world.

How do you react? What is your attitude like?

Do you moan and sulk or do you get on with it and say "No problem, I'll do it?"

When the coach asks you to help pick up the equipment at the end of a training session; do you pretend to do something else or mess around with your friend kicking the balls?

Think about the two different types of people we spoke about earlier.

What would the player with the good attitude do compared with what the player with the bad attitude would do?

What would you do?

"Do what is right not what is easy"

Summary

• Just like it takes effort, work, practice and patience to become a good player. It takes effort, work and practice to improve your attitude.

• You could say that people with a good positive attitude tend to make the best of things and people with a bad attitude tend to make the worst of things.

• To help you develop a great attitude you have to practice and be proactive (be brave and go first!)

• Be a "front seater", this means when the "Gaffa" is talking…Listen and be right at the front! One of our maxims is "Proximity is Power" – you have to be around the action to get in the action. Quite often we make our own "luck" simply by being in the right place at the right time.

• Model other people who you know have great attitudes, not just the ones who you think are "cool".

• Having a great attitude is not just for when times are good, a great attitude is most helpful when things aren't going your way. A great attitude can get you through the hardest of times.

• Invest the time to develop a great attitude and then spend the time looking after it. Attitude is just like any other "perishable skill", if you don't keep nurturing the skill, it will diminish over time…You have been warned!
Remember…

"Your attitude will determine your altitude!"

Onward to Chapter #2…

CHAPTER 2
PRACTICE

Success Secret #2
Practice

Practice -
The 4 keys to practice

1. **Dedication**
2. **Discipline**
3. **Determination**
4. **Daring!**

The 2nd secret may seem really obvious but without correct practice, the chances of you improving your skills are very low indeed.

The **"4 keys to practice"** is the only way that you can "**Earn**" the skills that will give you the freedoms to do what you really want to do.

The world is full of people who wanted to achieve their goals and dreams but because of one reason or another they didn't bother or their attitude wasn't great and they gave up.

These people weren't willing to put in the energy to do "**4 Key Practice**" and be free to do reach their dreams.

The world is also full of people who have **"Paid the price"**, and earned the freedoms to do whatever it was that they wanted to do.

I've heard it said that expecting to be brilliant and getting things instantly without putting the work in, is like saying to a fire, *"...give me some heat and then I'll put on the wood!'* Crazy! It doesn't work!

You must put the practice in!

What to practice...?

" *Persistent perfect practice produces perfect performance period.* "

Practice the right things.

When you next ask your coach…
"Can we play a game yet!?!"
Make sure that you have "earned" the game by practicing first!

" *...no one can do the work for you. You must do the work!* "

In any pursuit of skill or excellence, there are **"Fun" damentals** that you need to learn well.

Invest your time doing the basics really well and you won't go far wrong.

Yes, they can be boring and unexciting, but by practicing the basics and getting really good at them, you are making the tools that will allow you to be *a "Master" on the pitch*.

Fundamental skills are things like…

accurate passing, control, first touch, dribbling, running with the ball, heading, tackling, throw-in's, corners and of course shooting are really important.

Pro Coaching Football Academy are big fans of multiple sport activities. Judo and martial arts are excellent for core strength. Dance is an incredible discipline for agility, balance and coordination too.

Doing multiple sports means you can take many of the principles and disciplines back to football to create a unique blend of skill and concepts that will serve you well.

"*What you do in Private you will be rewarded for in Public* "

How to practice?

Here are a few tips on how to practice…

• *Prepare* – make sure that you are in the right mental and physical shape to practice. Get your equipment ready or have it out and ready to go. There is nothing worse than being in the "zone" and then having to stop to pump up your ball!

• *Plan* – Have a little plan in mind about what you are going to work on and what you would like to achieve from the practice. Set some goals, challenges and targets for yourself. Be sure to have an end time. Little and often is much better than one "ma-hoo-sive" session a week.

• *Plot* – make sure that you know what you have taken from the practice and write it down. This is really helpful when looking at your progress or areas that you might need to pay more attention to.

• Play – Have fun. Take your football seriously, but don't take yourself too seriously.

Practice and experiment with the tempo and intensity at which you practice. Practicing at **"Game Tempo"** for a period of time. Include lots of variety, some constant and some random practices to engage all parts of your brain and body.

"The players of the future will be self-learners. Coaches will be more like facilitators helping and guiding players" **- Mark Beauchamp**

When to practice?
Most of the players that we have had the pleasure to work with, never wanted to come off the field!
Think, there will be right times and wrong times to practice.
Listen to your body, be sensible with your commitments and priorities.
Talk with a parent, teacher, coach or manager to
help you come up with a training schedule.
Make a schedule. The benefits can be phenomenal. A well-structured schedule speeds up your development. Factoring breaks and rest periods.
If you are currently in a training programme, you need to be at the very least equalling the technical

elements of the programme in your own time. e.g. If you do 1 hour of technical practice in a programme then you need to be doing 1 hour of technical practice in your own time to practice what you have learned.

N.B. This rule of thumb doesn't hold fast for physical activity – be mindful of over play and burn out.

Who to practice with?

Mix it up! Solo practice is vitally important for your development as a player. Having said that we learn by copying so playing and practicing with talented players will be of huge benefit to you.

Remember...only copy the good stuff!

"...if you're the best player in your team, you're probably in the wrong team."

Play and practice with players who are older than you and younger than you. Play and practice with players who are slower and quicker than you. Really test yourself and give yourself a challenge, stay safe and make sure that you can physically cope.

Where to practice?

Be creative and safe! Football is a game that is played all over the world, and on lots of different surfaces and environments. Practice wherever is appropriate.

Vary the shapes and sizes that you practice on too. This will help develop a variety of skills and keep you very sharp. Sometimes uneven ground can be a good test for your reactions – just concentrate on keeping your ankles intact.

Try to have some structured practice with a team or a group as well as friendly kick abouts with your mates. The mixture of training will give you a broad spectrum of experiences too, all of which you can take with you in to the game.

Why practice?
Simple answer. To make mistakes! It may sound crazy but the more mistakes that you make and learn from, the better you will become. It has been scientifically proven that when we make a mistake our brains are stimulated more than when we get something right.

Don't get down on yourself for any mistakes, instead think, "Ah another chance to learn, adapt and get better!" Remember the players of the future will be self-learners and self- correctors. The players of the future will be able to evaluate their own performances and listen to others in order to improve and develop.

If you get the mix and balance of practice right, it can be a lot of fun. Work on the things you are good at, as well as the things that you need to get better at. The more time and effort you put into practice the more benefits, success and fun you will get from playing.
Enjoy it!

Summary

- Use the 4 Keys to Practice: Dedication, Discipline, Determination and Daring.
- Apply the "P's" – Prepare, Plan, Plot…and Play!
- Make mistakes, be brave enough to try new things.
- Practice intelligently. Excellence is not enough, you need to have wisdom too!
- Focus on the "fun" damentals – the basics. Do the simple things, well and do them quickly.
- Think – who, when, where, why, what and how questions when you practice…then answer the questions you ask!

Great footballers never stop learning so here is Chapter 3 all about…

CHAPTER 3

EDUCATION & LEARNING

Success secret #3
Education and Learning

The next secret is perhaps one of our favourites. Education & learning Why is education so important?

It's said that "Knowledge is Power", in our book…

"Knowledge is just that, Knowledge, until you mix it with passion, intelligence and action"

Once you have the right mix then education and learning are magnificent tools to help you experience the game at its fullest.

Great Teachers

Getting the very best teachers is one of the crucial ingredients to success in football. Notice that teachers is plural – no one person can know everything. If anyone tells you that they do then run…fast. For your development as a player you MUST have great teachers in every area.

The most important person in your own education is YOU! *You must take responsibility for your own learning and education*.

Every single one of the great players had good teachers around them to learn from and if they didn't have a good teacher, they found a teacher wherever they looked - learning from friends, other players, the TV, everywhere.

I knew a guy who taught himself to do "keepie uppies" with a conker! Can you imagine how good his ball control was!?! Now that's self-learning!

The thing about education is it is a two-way street, which means you have to want to learn. Your hunger

❝You must take responsibility for your own learning, no one can do it for you!❞

to learn more and more and then put what you have learned in to practice and action, will be the difference between success and failure. Take responsibility for your own learning!

Some ideas to spark your learning creativity…

Ok, what do you need to learn? Try some of these ideas…

Watching
Watching the game is a great way to learn! Watching the game on T.V. can help.

Watch a game with the sound turned off! It is a bit weird at first. You will soon start to watch the game in a different way and notice small things that perhaps you didn't notice before with the distraction of the commentary. It is not the same as watching the game as a fan, but you are watching to learn not just to enjoy.

❝*Make the distinction between being a student of the game and a fan of the game*❞

Go to "Live" games – there is nothing better than being at a "live" game to help you study the game.

You get to see the whole pitch and all of the players. When you watch though try not to get "fixated" by the ball. Watch what goes on away from the ball…you will be amazed!

Study one player - if you are lucky enough to have pause TV then you have a great advantage when studying players. With pause TV can stop and go back to see what the player did at different points in the game. Just studying one player will require some patience and is quite tricky at first. With a little practice, (there's that word again!), you will become a master!

> **"Don't watch the ball, just watch one specific player to see what he does when he is both on and off the ball "**

Top Tip - Watch the game as a player and a student and not just as a fan.

Reading
There are a multitude of great books about the beautiful game that will help you on your journey. Coaching Books, Magazines, Autobiographies can all be a part of your education and learning.

Youtube Videos
There is an invaluable amount of great football videos on youtube to help expand your mind. Remember a mind and an imagination that has been expanded can never go back to its previous state. Expanding your mind creates more space and more space means a bigger area to develop in. Think big!

Have a look on our youtube channel http://www.youtube.com/procfa if you can't find the topic that you want there, call us and we would be delighted to do a video on the subject for you.

Asking – Interviews and questions

One of the oldest surviving books has some "sage-like" knowledge that says, "ask and you shall receive…". It's true!

If you don't know something and you want to know it, Ask!

Most people don't ask because they are too scared or feel stupid. If you want to know an answer ask someone who already has the knowledge – it could be the catalyst to the future of your dreams.

> **" The man who asks a question is a fool for a minute, the man who does not ask is a fool for life. "**
> –Confucius

Have a couple of great questions ready to ask at all times. Start thinking about them now. If you could meet your footballing hero what would you ask them?

> **" Great questions produce Great answers! "**

Where to find help?

Here is a little advert for you too. **Get a great coach to help with your education.** The coach that you choose should be experienced enough to help you to a certain level and then help you find a coach who can take you on to the next level.

When you are looking for a team to join or a coaching programme ask tough questions! Questions like what is your playing philosophy? How do you think you can best help me? Where do I need to improve? Where do you see me playing in 5 years?

All of the answers that the coach gives, will provide you with valuable information about who and where the right place is for you. You can get in touch with Pro coaching Football Academy at any time and we would be delighted to help you. Info@procoachingfootballacademy.com

If you do take responsibility for your education and you are in charge of your education then you will have an exciting journey ahead!

> ❝ *I wouldn't give a fig for simplicity on this side of complexity but I would give my right arm for simplicity on the other side of complexity!* ❞

This quote for our purposes means that quite often when you learn something you end up back where you started but with greater skills and the difference is, you have valuable experience that you have picked up on the learning journey.

One other way of explaining this is:

I can show you how to kick a ball, but unless you have tried it yourself, made a few mistakes, adjusted, practiced and developed, you will never truly know how to kick a ball properly.

> ❝ *You have to do the work, no-one can do it for you, and that is a good thing too!* ❞

Summary

• Take responsibility for your own learning
• Develop a huge appetite for learning
• Ask lots of brilliant questions
• Apply what you learn
• Keep a record of what you learn for the future
• Become a student of the game as well as a fan – it's different being a student.

Education and learning is nothing without Chapter #4…

Success Secret #4
Health and fitness

Health and fitness is one of the big secrets – without health and supreme fitness your chances of super success in football are limited to say the least.

The ancient Roman Gladiators had a saying *"mens sana in corpore sano"*, which roughly translates – *Healthy Mind Healthy Body*. Even the mighty Romans "back in the day", knew the importance of looking after themselves.

What is health and fitness and what is the difference? Is there a difference? The answer seems to be a yes and no. Confusing huh!?! The two are totally joined. You can be fit and not healthy and you can be healthy and not fit.

The best option for sports people is a good balance of the two. Look after your fitness by placing appropriate demands upon your body to grow the body's ability to perform at the top levels. Running and things like Yoga would be good examples. Keep your body healthy by ensuring it has the right environments to be able to perform.

Great examples would be eating the right foods and getting right amount of sleep.

The benefits to your confidence when you are fit and healthy are immeasurable too.

> " *You may have to sacrifice something that's good, like watching a late game on T.V. for something that's better like going to bed early to get a good night's sleep before your big game the next day!* "

> " *Healthy mind Healthy body!* "

Conditioning your body so that it can perform at peak levels is vital. Being in peak physical shape not only means that you will perform on the pitch well, it also means that you can deal with the demands of the game better and bounce back from injury and fatigue quicker.

One of the challenges for younger players is finding the right balance between training and playing. The combination of over play and too much training can actually have a negative effect. In the same respect too much game play and not enough training isn't ideal either. When you are tired things seldom look or feel good, *rest and sleep (nature's miracle)*, is a vital part of the Health and Fitness element.

Educate yourself about health and fitness. There is a lot of conflicting information around health and fitness so you may find applying the "model T" thinking tool really helpful (see page 6). You are unique so getting to know your body and "listening" to your body is vital on the health and fitness journey.

The rules of thumb that we have put together for you at Pro Coaching we call the…

"S" for success formula. Here it is…

• **Strength** – Having good overall body strength will serve you well during the game, in training and help defend you against injury. Depending upon your age, your own body weight is enough to develop the strength that you require to play the game.

• **Sleep** – Without doubt sleep is nature's miracle. During sleep our minds and bodies repair and are rejuvenated. Make getting the correct amount of rest and sleep a priority in your quest for health and fitness.

• **Sustenance** – In computer speak there is an expression GIGO, which means "garbage in, garbage out". Simply translated it means if you put garbage coding into the computer then you will get garbage out! The same holds true for our bodies. If you are constantly putting rubbish in via the food and drink that passes your lips then you can only expect to get garbage performance and garbage results out. This garbage can come in the forms of lack of energy and becoming susceptible

to illnesses. Take good care of your body and respect it and it will serve you well. The same principle applies to you what you put in to your mind so be "mindful" about what you listen to, watch and say…your mind is always taking in information! You get more of what you focus on, so focus on the good stuff.

• **Suppleness** – This component goes hand in hand with Strength and Stamina. Football requires a very demanding mix on the body's "aerobic" (with air) and anaerobic (without air) systems to provide the energy required. Training in a variety different ways helps us develop these systems and keep them in tip top shape. The benefits of being supple and flexible will help all of the Super "S's" of health and fitness. Famously Ryan Giggs is a massive fan of Yoga, a very ancient practice

that helps to keep your body in tip top shape. There must be something in it as Ryan Giggs has had an incredible career well in to his 40's! Try simple stretches and movements so that your body has a full range of movement in every department. Suppleness in your mind is also important, so remember to keep your mind flexible too .

• **Speed** – Football requires an ability to be quick, most of the time over quite short distances. Practicing short sprints in different directions over various distance can be really helpful to improve your speed. Focus on taking off on different legs. Games like tag are brilliant for developing your speed. Think about timing yourself or challenging yourself against other people who are just quicker than you, you will soon develop the speed and knowledge to catch them over time with practice.

• **Stamina-** There are different types of stamina including mental and physical types. Stamina is our ability to keep going over time with certain demands put upon us. You can develop your physical stamina with repetitive practices over longer periods of time. Running and Jogging are good activities to develop your aerobic (with air) stamina. Sprinting is a good way to develop your anaerobic (without air) stamina. You can tell which ability you are using simply by noticing your breathing and your ability to hold a conversation. Using your aerobic capacity you will be able to hold a reasonable conversation. Using your anaerobic capacity you will struggle to hold a conversation.

• **Smiles –** The master key in the S for Success formula. There will be good times and not so good times on your football journey but the most important thing is that you really enjoy yourself and learn to appreciate the ups and the downs too. Smile often you will be amazed at what it will do for you and your team around you. Try it now…**smile**.

Summary

• Healthy Mind & Healthy Body
• Research
• Have a health and fitness programme
• Use the S's as guide
• Smile

Which brings us neatly on to our next chapter, Chapter 5…

CHAPTER 5

TEACHING & SHARING

Success Secret #5
Teaching and Sharing

Teaching, sharing and helping others is one of the quickest ways to football success. All players who come to Pro Coaching are asked to teach what they have learned at the session to a friend within the next 24 hours. Why do that? Read on and find out…

When you teach someone else, magic literally happens in your brain and body. The act of teaching others helps you too…

• **Remember!** Because you have to go over the skills that you learned again and your brain searches for the memory of what you already know. This "Remembering" strengthens the memory bonds in your mind which makes it easier to use the skill the next time you need it. The really good news is that by remembering a skill you are actually helping it to switch to auto pilot. Repetition is the mother of skill.

• **Repeat!** Repetition is the mother of skill. When you teach you are repeating what you already know which means that you get to do it

again. Top Tip! Your mind doesn't know the difference between something real and something that is imagined – so the more that you go over one of your skills even in your mind you will get better at it! Brilliant news.

• **Get really really good** – When you are teaching a skill to someone else you have to think about the skill in a different way. Teaching makes you break down a skill in to smaller parts and then put it back togetter again. Teaching gives you a deep knowledge of how and why some things work and something's don't work. This is good news because thinking about things in a different way gives you more information and more information helps you solve more problems and come up with better solutions. Teaching also means that you add the stuff that you already know to the new stuff making it even more effective, so... Teaching makes you even cleverer than you already are! Now that is cool!

• **Rejoice** – I couldn't think of a better "R" word! When you teach someone how to do something and they get it and get better at it, they feel good. When your friends feel good, you feel good, and when you feel good you learn more effectively and you can carry out tasks more effectively too...like playing football! Teaching is very very cool.

• **Review** – When you teach you have to review all that you know. Thinking about different ways to explain and help other people understand, helps you understand things at a much deeper level too.

❝ *...a word to the wise!*

People who teach tend to be able to learn more, more quickly.

Our advice? If you want to become better at **❞** *something then teach it!*

Find the best teachers!

Find the best footballing teachers that you can...there are some great teachers at Pro Coaching Football Academy to learn from :0)

Summary

• Teach what you learn within 24 hours
• Share your ideas with others
• Think about how you would teach what you are learning now to someone else...even if it is to the dog!
• Study and Learn these R's, and then put them into to practice.
"...let's get some "Support" as we move to the penultimate chapter... success secret #6...

CHAPTER 6

YOUR TEAM

Success Secret #6
Your Team

No one to date has ever been successful on their own. Have a little think about all of the great players that you know. Think about your favourite players. They all have one thing in common they have a great team around them.

Who is on your team? How do you treat them? What do they do for you and what do you do for them?

" Top Tip - Build a great team "

Having a great team around you is a necessity if you want to be super successful at football. We are not just talking about the players in our team, (although they are important too). We are talking about the team that supports you.

Professional footballers often have an army of people to help and support them, coaches, physio's, agents, fitness trainers and dieticians, advisors, managers this list can go on and on.

You probably already have a great team around you that you just haven't thought about. Take a minute to think about who is on your team at the moment...

The people who look after you –
Your parents or carers.

• Your family
• Your friends
• Your coach or managers
• Your teachers
• Your doctor
You could say that everyone is
supporting you in some way!

Ok so you have a team around you

even though you perhaps haven't
thought about it in that way. Let's
give you a few tips to creating
a team to help you get super
successful in football.

**Top Tip - Choose your team
very carefully.**

The reason that we say very
carefully is because choosing the
right people for your team can make

all of the difference to your success. They need to be people who have your best interests at heart and are not just in it for themselves.

The people on your team need to be experts or at least on the journey to become experts. The people on your team need to be qualified. This doesn't mean that they have bits of paper qualifications coming out of their ears, but it does mean that they have a proven track record of success and experience in their field.

"Good News! It's your team!" – "Bad News! It's your team!"

You need to take responsibility for your team.

No one will ever care about your success as much as you. Remember this when working with your team. Take responsibility and look after your team, NEVER blame them! If things are going wrong then get creative and guide and lead your team to success.

"Love your family – choose your team!"

Sharing your vision

Share your vision and dreams with your "carefully chosen" team members. I say carefully chosen team members because, you don't want to share you dream with someone who will laugh and ridicule your vision of success. You really want to share your dream with someone who will be supportive of your dream, but also realistic too.

"The best people to share your vision of success are people you trust, respect and you know will tell you the truth even if the truth is something that you don't want to hear!"

Why would you want to share your dreams and visions with someone else?

Sharing you dream and vision with the right carefully chosen people helps everyone pull in the right direction. Sharing the goal also helps the team to support you in the right ways through good times and bad times.

Finding your team

Write down a list of all of the roles of the people you would like on your team, then start putting names next to the roles. You don't have to show anyone your list and you can always change it at a later date.

Remember sometimes your friends are not the best people to have on your success team. They can still be your friends but they are just not on your success team.

"*Choose your friends, Love your family, Nurture and look after your team.*"

Summary

• Develop a Dream Team
• Look after your team – they are as important as you!
• Love your family, choose your team!

let's create the future with the final success secret for now success secret #7

◀- - - - -▶

CHAPTER 7

VISION PLANS & GOALS

Success Secret #7
Visions, Plans and Goals, Goals, Goals!

What is your vision? What do you think the journey to football success will look like?

Have some fun for a few minutes, close your eyes and just dream about the journey. Get in as much detail as possible. What is it that you really want? What is it like? What do you want to achieve from your time in the game?

You probably just want to have a lot of fun and that is brilliant. Here is one of the biggest secrets though... there is more! You can have much more than fun by playing football. If you apply yourself to these secrets then by default you have to grow and develop.

You really hold the keys to your own happiness, success and destiny. Is it possible by just following a few simple rules? The answer seems to be "Yes", but you must find out for yourself.

> **" It's not in the "doing" of these secrets to success, it is the person you become by applying yourself as you practice them "**

Who you become determines what you do and what you do determines what you have and what you have determines what you can give.

"Be - Do - Have - Give"

Invest some time in to deciding what it is that you really want and then get on working hard towards your goal.

Map out your vision, don't worry about making it perfect you can change it as you go as long. Keep the end in mind. It will be a real help for you.

Putting your vision on paper is like having a "SatNav" to help you get to your destination.

The super cool thing is that you can change the route on the map anytime you want and still end up where you want to go!

Write your vision down now and look at it every day. Have fun creating your vision.

For the Journey

On your journey, make little targets to aim for as you travel on your way to your goals and **celebrate** when you have hit these small targets and goals.

Visualising, planning and setting goals helps to provide you with "Wisdom" for your journey to football success.

Remember what we said earlier – "excellence is not enough on its own; you must have wisdom too

Your Philosophy – Big Word Alert!

One way to make it easy to understand what philosophy is, could be to think of your philosophy as your mode of transport that you will travel in, as you journey towards your goals. Your vision is what the journey will look like as you travel.

Do you want to make the journey as hard as possible? Easy as possible?

Developing a great philosophy will help you on your football journey. Your philosophy will help or hinder you when your car breaks down, when you take a wrong turn, when you run out of petrol. This may sound pessimistic but bad things happen to everyone, even sports people! No-one gets away with it!

Your Philosophy will also help or hinder you when things are going really well too. It can keep your feet on the ground and stop you getting big headed and arrogant to a fault. Don't confuse confidence with arrogance – the two are totally different!

Summary

- Take time to think and dream

- Share your dream and vision with trusted members of your team

- Decide how you are going to travel (your philosophy)

- Celebrate your successes

- Learn from any feedback –Wisdom

- Enjoy the journey as much as the destination

- Be – Do – Have – Give

- Write down your vision. Look at your vision and act on it every day.

Part of our philosophy at Pro Coaching Football Academy is…

"It's not what happens to us that counts it's how we react to the things that happen to us that count. You always have a choice, even if it's choosing how to feel about what has happened."

Final Thoughts for now…

So now you have read the 7 secrets to football success. They are not really secrets because this information is available to everyone. The real secrets are only found in the doing and the practicing of all of the 7 secrets together.

Look closely at any successful player or top sports person that you know and they will have all demonstrated these secrets during their rise to the top.

All of these secrets are "transferable skills". Developing these skills and secrets with have a huge impact in all areas of your life. Dedicate and invest time studying them and they will serve you well.

We hope that you have enjoyed reading about some of the secrets to football success. If you would like to learn more and as one of the secrets is education, get in touch with us at pro coaching and we look forward to helping you on your football journey.

Mark Beauchamp and the entire "multiple award winning" pro coaching football academy team

"Genius and excellence are not enough by themselves you must have wisdom too!"

The Pro Coaching Seven Secrets to Super Football Success check list

Success Secret	Doing ok	Needs work	Notes
Attitude			
Practice			
Education & learning			
Health & fitness			
Teaching & Sharing			
Support and your team			
Your Team			
Vision Plans & Goals			

Pro Coaching Football Academy

"Responsible custodians of our future leaders"

"A "multiple award winning" friendly Professional independent, impartial, gold standard player development resource for all players, parents, coaches, managers and educators."

"Service through Excellence"

"Developing Players and People from the inside out"

- Professional Academy level football training sessions for all ages
- Team Academy sessions
- Professional school holiday football programmes
- Individual player pre pro club academy entrance assistance
- Football Events
- Expert School Curriculum and After School Provisions (Ofsted)
- School Enterprise through Sport and Business provider
- The genius programme – getting learners back on track
- 1st for Sport delivery of Leadership through football programme
- Fund raising events
- Bubble football experts
- Team Building Events
- Birthday party celebrations
- Inspirational & motivational speaking
- Football education media resources
- Football Educational Books and Resources
- Expert football development advice
- Team, Game and training analysis
- Bespoke educational packages for players/teams/managers/coaches/educators
- Educational Talks and Presentations
- Educational Football Book Authors
- Training and development award winners

AWARDS
2012 - Training & Development - Best Business
2013 - Small Business of the year
2014 - Best Business in education

Bulk orders for clubs and schools
Discounts are available for clubs and teams ordering bulk quantities, please contact Pro Coaching Football Academy directly via the details below. A number of complimentary copies are also available for schools and educational establishments.

Training and Education
Coaching sessions for individual players, whole teams, coaches, managers, teachers and parents are available upon request. These valuable sessions are bespoke designed to individual needs and requirements. Please contact us for more details.

Speaking and Appearances
Mark Beauchamp is available for key note speaking engagements and appearances. Please contact Head Office for availability and fees.

Press Information
For all TV, Radio and Online Multimedia communications please contact head Office directly via the office@procoachingfootballacademy.com email address.

Pro Coaching Football Academy contact details
Head Office: 36 Kingfisher Drive, Littlehampton, West Sussex, BN17 7GX
Tel: 01903 718 400
Email: info@procoachingfootballacademy.com
Web: http://www.procoachingfootballacademy.com
Facebook: http://www.facebook.com/procoachingfootballacademy Twitter: http://www.twitter.com/procfa
Youtube: http://www.youtube.com/procfa